PRAYERS
for a WIDOW'S
JOURNEY

GAYLE ROPER

HARVEST HOUSE PUBLISHERS
EUGENE, OREGON

Published in association with Books & Such Literary Management, www.booksandsuch.com.

Cover design by Studio Gearbox

Cover images © Jim Ward Morris / Artville CD; Irtsya, Artnizu / Shutterstock

Interior design by Chad Dougherty

For bulk, special sales, or ministry purchases, please call 1-800-547-8979. Email: CustomerService@hhpbooks.com

PRAYERS *for a* WIDOW'S JOURNEY
Copyright © 2024 by Gayle Roper
Published by Harvest House Publishers
Eugene, Oregon 97408
www.harvesthousepublishers.com

ISBN 978-0-7369-8894-0 (pbk)
ISBN 978-0-7369-8895-7 (eBook)

Library of Congress Control Number: 2023938675

Printed in Colombia

23 24 25 26 27 28 29 30 31 32 / NI / 10 9 8 7 6 5 4 3 2 1

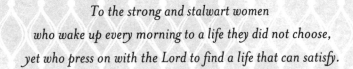

To the strong and stalwart women
who wake up every morning to a life they did not choose,
yet who press on with the Lord to find a life that can satisfy.

You let men ride over our heads;
we went through fire and through water;
but you brought us out to a place of abundance.

Psalm 66:12

...though our outer self is wasting away...

I am a displaced person, Father, a refugee, an alien trying to grasp the customs and nuances of my new homeland. I never wanted this life upheaval, but a war broke out. There were no guns or missiles or IEDs in my war. Rather, I faced illness and brokenness and death.

I may not be trudging the road with my belongings on my back or tied to the roof of my car, but I am wandering as disoriented as any refugee from violence. May I not lose heart, Father God, as I choose to trust You to renew me day by difficult day.

_____

_____

_____

_____

So we do not lose heart.
Though our outer self is wasting away,
our inner self is being renewed day by day.

2 Corinthians 4:16

...I will not leave you comfortless...

There's a gigantic hole, Lord. A cavern. An abyss, empty and black. Ugly.

That may sound like overkill, like overstatement, but is it? The large part of me that my husband filled with his love and his presence has been ripped away. I look the same. I sound the same. I am not the same. The married part of me has disappeared. Poof! Gone. All that's left is silence and pain.

What will fill that gaping chasm that used to teem with life and love and purpose? Only You, Lord. Only You who will never leave me comfortless.

_____

_____

_____

_____

I will not leave you comfortless: I will come to you.

JOHN 14:18 KJV

...heal me, O LORD...

I'm so disappointed, Lord. You didn't heal him. You took him. You didn't have to. You are Jehovah-Rapha, the God who heals. But you didn't heal despite our prayers. I had to watch him fade away in front of me. Oh, I know he would have died sometime—we all will—but did it have to be now? I need him. Our children need him. Our grandchildren need him.

But You said no. You said You are all I need. All we need. I'm choosing to trust even though I don't understand. Now, will you please heal us in our grief?

Heal me, O LORD, and I shall be healed;
save me, and I shall be saved,
for you are my praise.

JEREMIAH 17:14

...when I remember you upon my bed...

Lord, I am alone in our wide, wide bed. If I sleep on his side, will I feel closer to him? I move over, cuddle into the pillow that still smells of him, but no. I am still alone in what is now *my* wide, wide bed.

During the day I can keep busy and redirect my thoughts. But in the dark of night in this bed we shared, where we talked, whispered, loved, and even turned our backs, I feel alone.

Lord, please hold me. I need to feel Your arms about me for the night is dark indeed.

When I remember you upon my bed,
and meditate on you in the watches of the night;
for you have been my help.

Psalm 63:6-7

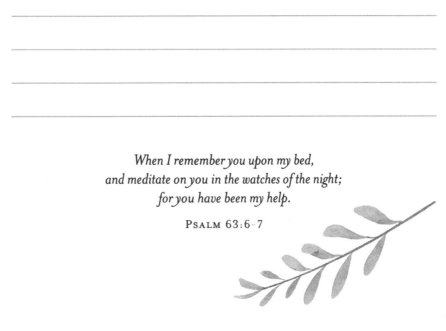

...when I am afraid...

Lord, how easy it is to imagine all that could go wrong. My money won't be enough. My car will break down. My health will fail. My family will be too busy for me. My friends will forget me. My church won't care about me. I'll grow old alone and always be alone. And then there are the big issues like war and famine, global warming and natural disasters. Evil.

Remind me, Lord, that even if my worst fears come true, You are always there. No, not *there*. *Here*, beside me. With me. I can put my trust in You.

When I am afraid, I put my trust in you.
In God, whose word I praise,
in God I trust; I shall not be afraid.
What can flesh do to me?

PSALM 56:3-4

...will not walk in darkness...

Lord, I'm caught in that widow's fog people talk about. It's like a white mist swirling about me, making the world vague. It surrounds me the same way I see pictures of real fog shrouding a mountaintop or enveloping a valley. I can't see through the emotional mists. I can't think clearly to make the choices and decisions that my situation requires. Voices, often frustrated with me, come as if from a distance.

I want to do what's wise and right if I can only decipher what that is. Help me see through the mists, O Lord. Let the light of the Son burn away the fog.

_____

_____

_____

_____

I am the light of the world. Whoever follows me
will not walk in darkness, but will have the light of life.

JOHN 8:12

...*not neglecting to meet together*...

Lord, I sit in church and watch all the couples. One laughs softly together. Another sits shoulder to shoulder. The stiff posture of those two telegraphs their anger. Did they have an argument on the way? We used to be all those couples: loving, agreeing and disagreeing, our two hearts one, even on the bad days. It's not the fault of the still-couples that they make my heart ache.

I've come broken into this ark of worship with all the two by twos. Help me remember that even in community, worship is the act of one with One. I still qualify.

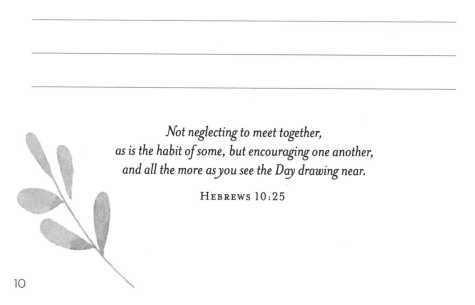

Not neglecting to meet together,
as is the habit of some, but encouraging one another,
and all the more as you see the Day drawing near.

HEBREWS 10:25

…*hear the voice of my pleas*…

Most days loving him wasn't a hard choice. He was a loveable and loving man. But there were the days I'd shake my head. *Really? Him?* I don't doubt he had days thinking the same about me. But we loved. Fiercely.

Now that he's gone, what do I do with the love I used to lavish on him? How do I manage without the love he freely gave me? How do I learn to live with this gnawing emptiness that was once filled with being us?

O Lord, hold me tight lest I break under the burden of my loss.

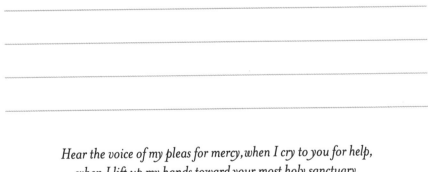

*Hear the voice of my pleas for mercy, when I cry to you for help,
when I lift up my hands toward your most holy sanctuary.*

PSALM 28:2

...the valley of the shadow of death...

I went shopping today, Lord, and it seemed strange to do something so normal. The very ordinariness of pulling cans from the shelves and bags from the freezers felt somehow disrespectful. I have become a widow. How can I be checking the price of apples? Do I care about the price of apples?

I thought the valley of the shadow meant his illness and his death. I didn't realize I would walk this valley for weeks, months, even years. But by Your grace, Lord, I will walk with confidence for You are with me.

Even though I walk through the valley of the shadow of death,
I will fear no evil, for you are with me.

PSALM 23:4

...to give you a future...

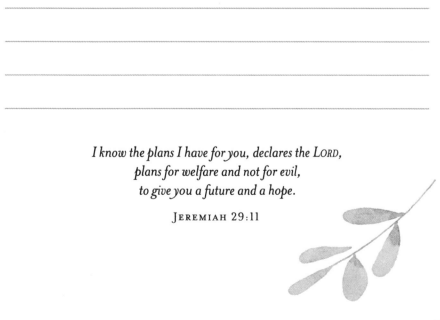

Lord, right now I don't want a future. I want my past. I want my husband. I want our life together. In memory, it glows golden. Beckoning. And I want it!

Of course I know it wasn't perfect. We had our bad days, our hard times. I also know I can't have it back no matter how I yearn for it. Part of my longing to go back is because I'm uncertain, even afraid of what lies ahead. But ahead lies the opportunity to trust in You to give me a fulfilling future. Ahead lie Your plans. Ahead lies life.

I know the plans I have for you, declares the LORD,
plans for welfare and not for evil,
to give you a future and a hope.

JEREMIAH 29:11

...for I am lonely and afflicted...

Lord, what do I do without him? We did everything together. Well, not everything. He had his job and I had mine, but we spent our free time together. "Isn't it wonderful they're so close," everyone said. They laughed at us because we held hands and finished each other's sentences.

Well, now I'm alone, and I don't know what to do without him. Weekends are the worst. How do I fill Saturday? We used to go places together, everything from the grocery store to the movies, regular places but always together. And Sunday? Church is so hard, the afternoon and evening so long.

Help me, Lord!

Turn to me and be gracious to me,
for I am lonely and afflicted.
The troubles of my heart are enlarged;
bring me out of my distresses.

PSALM 25:16-17

...but the Spirit himself intercedes...

Lord, I'm having difficulty forming any coherent prayer. Words tumble about in my mind, but they won't shape into rational thoughts or logical sentences. I reach for You in great need—a crying child with arms upraised—but I can't articulate what I feel, what I want.

When I'm with people, I manage words about daily things, ordinary things, but when it's just You and me? Not even white noise. I'm clinging to the thought that the Holy Spirit is interpreting my heart, saying what I cannot, when all I can manage is, "Jesus!"

But that's enough, isn't it, Lord? You are enough.

_____

_____

_____

_____

Likewise the Spirit helps us in our weakness.
For we do not know what to pray for as we ought,
but the Spirit himself intercedes for us
with groanings too deep for words.

ROMANS 8:26

...but God's firm foundation stands...

All I want to do, Lord, is thread this needle. I've threaded needles forever, but this one won't cooperate. Is it because I can't see the eye clearly with my eyes swollen from tears? Is it because my hand is shaking with the thought that I'll never thread a needle to sew for him again? No tiny shirt buttons. No split trouser seams.

The eye of the needle is the same as it ever was. The thread is the same. What's changed is me. My life. My everything. Remain my firm foundation, Lord. Be my constant, my support when I can't even do ordinary tasks.

_____

_____

_____

_____

But God's firm foundation stands, bearing this seal:
"The Lord knows those who are his."

2 TIMOTHY 2:19

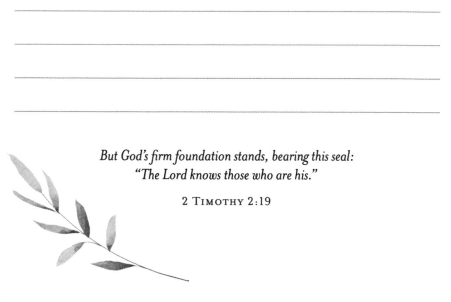

…out of my distress…

"Sit with me," he said. I looked at him, my arms full of laundry. "Let me get this washing started," I said, "and I'll be right back." I got sidetracked, and when I finally returned, he'd fallen asleep.

I promised myself I'd sit with him later, but the next thing I knew, the day was gone. And the next. And the next. Then he was gone.

I should have sat with him. He was far more important than the things that distracted me. Lord, I feel so guilty, so distressed at my poor choices. Forgive me for failing him and You.

_____

_____

_____

_____

Out of my distress I called on the Lord;
the Lord answered me and set me free.

PSALM 118:5

...we utter our Amen to God...

Lord, in my childhood church saying amen meant the amen-er agreed with whatever the pastor said. In the Bible when Ezra read the Scriptures to the congregation for the first time since their return from captivity, all the people cried, "Amen!" and fell on their knees in worship.

It's easy to say amen and agree when something good has happened. But it is so hard to agree with You when hard things happen! He's gone. My heart aches. How can I say amen?

Wait! It's not to his death that I must say amen, but to Jesus who sustains me through the loss.

_____

_____

_____

_____

All the promises of God find their Yes in him.
That is why it is through him
that we utter our Amen to God for his glory.

2 Corinthians 1:20

...rooted and built up in him...

I have several philodendrons, Father, the hardiest of plants that even my benign neglect can't kill. I frequently take cuttings and stick them in water to take root. I've one such cutting on my kitchen windowsill now. In one of Your amazing orchestrations, a healthy cluster of roots will grow, ready to be planted.

Father, a good root system is what I need in these harsh days of grief. I fear the pain-fueled winds of despair might topple me otherwise. May my roots dig down deep in You, so I stand strong against the storms of sorrow that batter me.

*As you received Christ Jesus the Lord, so walk in him,
rooted and built up in him and established in the faith.*

Colossians 2:6-7

...if the Lord had not been my help...

The house is so quiet, Lord. When the children were little, it reverberated with love and laughter, action and adrenaline. In time the kids grew and left us. We loved it when they came to visit, bringing their vitality and excitement. We loved it when they left, and we could catch our breath again.

Now he has left too, and the silence is overwhelming. He will never call me from the other room, asking me to bring him a drink while I'm up. And maybe the pretzels too? Or the Oreos?

Please keep me company, Lord, and fill the silence with Your presence.

If the Lord had not been my help,
my soul would soon have lived in the land of silence.

Psalm 94:17

...you will be like a well-watered garden...

Today is a hard day, Lord. My soul feels parched and dried up. I'm a flower struggling to grow in a crack in the road with the sun beating down on me and no rain in sight. I'm a little fir seedling fighting to survive after a fire has devastated my forest. I'm the houseplant no one's watered in weeks. I'm desiccated, Lord. Spent. Shriveled.

You say You're going to make me a well-watered garden? I know You can do anything, but You have a lot of work to do here, Gardener of my soul. Teach me to bloom for Your glory in spite of my drought.

_____

_____

_____

_____

You will be like a well-watered garden,
like a spring whose waters never fail.

ISAIAH 58:11 NIV

...whose hope is in the Lord his God...

The sky is overcast today, Lord, a study in shades of gray. The clouds part, and an irregular opening appears with beautiful blue showing through. Surrounding the opening is a rim of white clouds. It reminds me of an agate sliced open to reveal its glorious and colorful interior.

Slowly the opening of blue disappears, and gray once again dominates. Grief feels like this, Lord: gray, gray, gray, a splash of hope and color, gray, gray, gray. Guide my heart and my thoughts so that the breaks in the clouds become longer and the hope in my heart becomes stronger.

Blessed is he whose help is the God of Jacob,
whose hope is in the Lord his God,

PSALM 146:5

...do not be frightened...

Lord, I'm playing a lot of solitaire because, as I contemplate the cards, I don't have to think about how scared I am. I'm escaping my fear in the game, which is a valid strategy when things are overwhelming—as long as I don't fall into destructive escapism like drinking, compulsive shopping, or sleeping all day and watching TV all night.

As much as I appreciate solitaire or a novel with a guaranteed happy ending as a momentary tension reliever, I know there's a better escape, a safer place. A perfect hiding place from fear. May I escape to You, Lord, for it's You who will give me courage when I'm afraid.

Be strong and courageous.
Do not be frightened, and do not be dismayed,
for the LORD your God is with you wherever you go.

JOSHUA 1:9

…he gives to all of them their names…

There was a meteor shower last night, Lord. I searched the sky. Between the clouds and the lights of civilization I saw nothing.

But I saw meteor showers when we vacationed on a lake in Canada far from anywhere. We took our blankets and lay on the dock. The Milky Way blazed overhead and the aurora borealis sometimes danced on the northern horizon. We watched for the star streaks across the sky. There! There! It was amazing.

I now live a no-meteor life, Lord, but You, the star-maker and namer of stars, are my God. Remember my name. Heal my heart.

He heals the brokenhearted and binds up their wounds.
He determines the number of the stars;
he gives to all of them their names.

PSALM 147:3-4

...I have loved you with an everlasting love...

I'm watching TV, Lord. It's cold tonight, and I'm wrapped in a cozy throw against the encroaching chill. It's a lovely throw, soft and pretty. It even has my name embroidered across one corner. It's large, easily covering me from throat to toes. It's keeping me warm, and I'm thankful for it.

But I used to be wrapped in his arms to ward off life's chill. It was warm there, safe there. Sigh. While my body is comfortable under my throw, my heart shivers with loss and loneliness. Wrap the comforter of your everlasting love about me, Lord. Warm my chilled and hurting heart.

_____

_____

_____

_____

I have loved you with an everlasting love;
therefore I have continued my faithfulness to you.

JEREMIAH 31:3

...the LORD gave...

Lord, the Boston fern is dying. It's the one I was given when my husband died. Then it was full and vibrant, fronds exploding in a fountain of green. It screamed health and life. I've cared for it, watered it, fed it. I've kept it in the right light. I've done everything I'm supposed to do, and still it's dying.

I know it sounds crazy, Lord, but it's as if he's dying again. I couldn't keep him alive either, no matter how hard I tried. Of course, I can replace the fern, but he's irreplaceable.

Give me the grace to say, "Blessed be the name of the Lord."

_____

_____

_____

_____

The LORD gave, and the LORD has taken away;
blessed be the name of the LORD.

JOB 1:21

...create in me...

I've read about phantom pain when a limb is amputated. The severed nerves make it seem as if the missing body part is present and aching.

I feel like an amputee, Lord, only it's not a limb I've lost. It's my heart. It's like it's no longer there. I'm experiencing only the ache in my chest where it used to be.

Of course, it is there, traitorous thing, beating as if nothing happened. Ba-dum, ba-dum, ba-dum. David prayed for a clean heart, Lord. How about a new heart that doesn't ache? Or would You rather renew a right spirit in my grieving and pain-filled heart?

_____

_____

_____

_____

Create in me a clean heart, O God,
and renew a right spirit within me.

PSALM 51:10

...do not keep silence...

He used to say nice things to me, Lord. "You look pretty." "You did a good job." "That was a great meal." He used to ask good questions. "Why do you want to do that?" "Are you sure that's the best way?" "Why is that your responsibility?"

I miss that iron sharpening iron aspect of our marriage. It enriched me and stretched me. It made me a stronger, better person. Now where there was conversation and challenge, there is only resounding silence.

O Lord, come into my silence and give me life. Give me purpose. Give me noise.

O God, do not keep silence;
do not hold your peace or be still, O God!

PSALM 83:1

...for you were strangers in the land of Egypt...

I remember when we first married, Lord, and he no longer had to go home each night. He was home. We were home. It didn't matter whether we were living in that little apartment with two doors to the bathroom and no lock on either one or the starter home we somehow never left. Together was home.

Now I'm homeless. Oh, I have a roof over my head, but the one who made it my home is gone. I'm an exile in my own house, a stranger in my version of Egypt. How grateful I am, Lord, that You love the stranger.

_____

_____

_____

_____

You shall treat the stranger who sojourns with you
as the native among you, and you shall love him as yourself,
for you were strangers in the land of Egypt:
I am the LORD your God.

LEVITICUS 19:34

...*if any of you lacks wisdom, let him ask...*

Lord, I'm having trouble with my car. It's reached the point of costing a goodly sum to pass inspection. So, what should I do? A new car? A used car? Keep this one and pay the repair bills?

You know that cars are not my strong suit. I'm not wired mechanically or scientifically. Whenever we bought a car, my responsibility was to pick the color and decide if the seats were comfortable—jobs for which I was fully qualified. Now I'm out of my depth, Lord. Please give me wisdom. Thank You for giving it generously and without reproach for my limitations.

_____

_____

_____

_____

If any of you lacks wisdom, let him ask God,
who gives generously to all without reproach,
and it will be given him.

JAMES 1:5

...we have this treasure in jars of clay...

Lord, I went to tai chi class today. It's an all-levels class, and much of it was repetitious for me. Still, it was wonderful. It made me move. It made me flex and bend. It helped me build strength and balance. It also made my neck crack, my shoulders ache, my thighs burn, and my lower back complain.

How limited I am, Lord, not only physically, as my class reminded me, but also mentally, emotionally, and spiritually. These very limitations are a gift from You—as is grief in its own way—because they force me to depend on You.

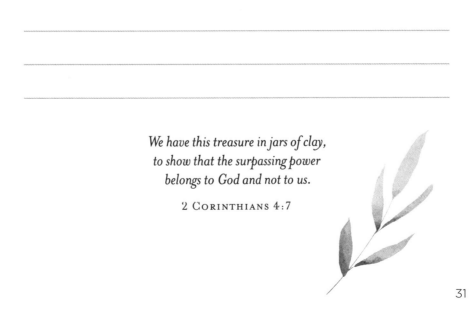

*We have this treasure in jars of clay,
to show that the surpassing power
belongs to God and not to us.*

2 Corinthians 4:7

…with her own hands…

Lord, I made a very foolish decision last night. I fell for the siren song of an infomercial and placed an order for a product that, in the light of day, looks of dubious benefit. I called my bank to stop payment, but they can't. The money had already been transferred.

If my husband had been here, I'd never have listened to the infomercial nor bought that product. His presence kept me grounded. Now I have to depend on myself, and I'm all too capable of doing something foolish. I don't expect to have wisdom and understanding beyond measure like Solomon, but, Lord, keep me from further folly.

The wise woman builds her house,
but with her own hands the foolish one tears hers down.

Proverbs 14:1 NIV

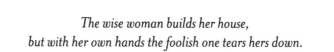

...as we also have forgiven...

What does a woman do, Lord, when she finds out her husband kept a secret from her? A widow shared with me that her husband was a good man who loved her, but to get his business through a tough patch, he borrowed against their house without telling her. He died suddenly. She learned his secret only when she tried to sell the house.

Forgiving a living person is hard, but forgiving someone who has died is a different kind of hard. There can be no explaining, no talking it through, no resolution to tumultuous emotions. She struggled, but she knew what God expected of her. She chose to forgive seventy times seven. Or more as needed.

_____

_____

_____

_____

Forgive us our debts,
as we also have forgiven our debtors.

Matthew 6:12

...*give unto the* LORD...

Lord, I'm looking at a watercolor I have hanging on the wall. Like many watercolors, the paint is a blurred wash, melding color into color. Because the artist is talented and in control, this blending is beautiful, balanced, satisfying.

My life feels blurred, Lord, and I don't think it's balanced or beautiful. My grief distorts. It robs me of light and shadow, hue and shading. It's as if I've become color-blind.

I don't want to live in tones of gray, Lord. I want my life to be a vibrant painting that reflects You in all Your beauty and holiness.

Give unto the LORD *the glory due unto his name:*
bring an offering, and come before him:
worship the LORD *in the beauty of holiness.*

1 CHRONICLES 16:29 KJV

...do not turn to the right or the left...

Lord, I travel these twisty Pennsylvania roads in sun and in storm, by daylight and by starlight. The berms are lined with signs that show the way the roads will bend.

My life has become a twisty, pain-filled road, Lord, and there are no convenient signs to warn me of an upcoming curve. What if I accidentally or intentionally turn off this life-road, reject it as Your path for me? Perhaps I'll discover an easier way to dilute or bury my ever-present pain. Alcohol. Drugs. Clubbing. Shopping. A man.

No, I choose Your way despite the twists and turns, the sadness and sorrow.

Do not turn to the right or the left;
keep your foot from evil.

PROVERBS 4:27 NIV

...nothing in all creation...

Lord, I'm at one end of a long tunnel, viewing everything and everyone from a distance. I'm disconnected, like there's a sheet of glass between me and the world. I see what's going on around me, but I can't touch it or it me. For someone who's used to engaging with people, here-but-not-here is strange and unnerving.

Lord, what a comfort to know that no matter how vague and lost I am, You are ever present. No matter how disconnected I feel, You hold me close. Thank You that nothing—not loss, not vagueness, not grief—can separate me from You.

_____

_____

_____

_____

I am convinced that...nothing in all creation
will ever be able to separate us from the love of God
that is revealed in Christ Jesus our Lord.

ROMANS 8:38-39 NLT

...for unto you is born this day...

The Christmas decorations are beginning to appear, Lord. They're pretty and shiny and depressing. The holidays are all about family, and our family has become Humpty Dumpty who can't be put back together again. The one who was central to us is missing. His chair is empty. His voice is silenced. His smile and encouragement are gone.

I need to remember what Christmas is really about, Lord, and it isn't family, wonderful as family may be. It's about Jesus, the Messiah, coming to offer salvation in the midst of my sorrow, the world's sorrow. Help me center my thoughts there, Lord.

---

*For unto you is born this day
in the city of David a Savior,
who is Christ the Lord.*

LUKE 2:11

...*revive us again*...

Lord, the poinsettias, my one concession to the season this first year, flourished for several weeks, giving color to my gray life. Now the brilliant red has crinkled to brown. The rich green is curling in on itself and falling. Their season is over.

Lord, these once vibrant plants mirror my experience. My life was busy, vital, and he filled it with color. Now my life-leaves are withering and my petals dropping. Our season is over, and I feel fit only for the compost heap.

Revive my soul, Lord, when I want to curl up and die. Help me face this new season bolstered by your unfailing love.

_____

_____

_____

_____

Will you not revive us again,
that your people may rejoice in you?
Show us your steadfast love, O Lord,
and grant us your salvation.

PSALM 85:6-7

...why are you cast down...

I stare at the stop sign, Lord. If there's one thing in life that is consistent, it's the stop sign. It's always a brilliant red with white edges and a large white STOP in the center. It's octagonal in shape and sits on its long black post at dangerous or busy intersections.

Why can't grief be like the stop sign, Lord? Why can't it hold its shape instead of shifting and changing by the day, the hour, the minute? Why can't it bring order instead of painful chaos?

And why can't it do what the sign says and STOP?

_____

_____

_____

_____

Why are you cast down, O my soul,
and why are you in turmoil within me?
Hope in God; for I shall again praise him, my salvation.

PSALM 42:5

...left all alone...

Lord, no one has touched me since he died. Oh, I've had many hugs from family and friends, but no one has held my hand. No one stood with an arm around me, pulling me close to his side. No one sat shoulder to shoulder, leaning into me as I leaned into him. No one rubbed my back or tugged me to rest against his chest.

This gift of casual touch is one intimacy, one security, one pleasure I lost when I lost him. What can possibly replace this right and privilege?

Nothing.

So I turn my heart to You, Lord. I set my hopes in You.

_____

_____

_____

_____

She who is truly a widow, left all alone,
has set her hope on God and continues
in supplications and prayers night and day.

1 TIMOTHY 5:5

...*whoever has the Son*...

Lord, I recently went to my favorite restaurant for a late lunch only to discover they had closed early. I walked away hungry.

I didn't plan on an early closing of our marriage either. I was left hungry for many more years. When the restaurant closed, I drove down the street to another and was fed. When our marriage ended, I could do nothing to resurrect it. No Lazarus moment for us.

But like Martha and Mary, I don't mourn without hope. You, Lord, are the resurrection and the life.

He believed in You and will never die. Not mere resurrection for him. Eternal life.

_____

_____

_____

_____

This is the testimony, that God gave us eternal life,
and this life is in his Son. Whoever has the Son has life;
whoever does not have the Son of God does not have life.

1 JOHN 5:11-12

...You knit me together...

When I was young, Lord, I knit a sweater for my husband, and somehow it ended up with batwings instead of sleeves. After all the time to make the thing, it took only a few minutes to unravel it so I could try again.

My life has unraveled, Lord. After all the time and work to weave our lives together in a satisfying pattern, everything has come undone. And the threads aren't wrapped in a neat ball to be easily reused. There are knots and tangles and pain. You knit me together before as babe, as bride, and as wife. Please take the damaged threads and knit me anew.

_____

_____

_____

_____

You knit me together in my mother's womb...
when I was woven together in the depths of the earth.

PSALM 139:13,15 NIV

...I will sing of your strength...

As You know, Lord, my husband had no sense of rhythm. If we clapped to a song in church, he had to choose to either sing or clap. He couldn't do both. And he didn't care.

Lord, I've lost my life's rhythm, and I care deeply. The cadence of my life has changed so greatly I can't find a new tempo. What had been a melody and inflection I knew and enjoyed has become a pattern both discordant and unfamiliar.

Father, teach me to sing a new song to You for You have been my refuge in my distress.

I will sing of your strength;
I will sing aloud of your steadfast love in the morning.
For you have been to me a fortress
and a refuge in the day of my distress.

PSALM 59:16

...*that no bitter root grows up*...

"I spent forty-three years married to someone who didn't love me," she says. "Oh, he never abused me physically, but I felt abused emotionally by the very absence of his consideration, his affection, his respect. He did as he pleased financially with no concern for my feelings or our family's needs.

"Now he's gone, and I fight constant bitterness at the chaos he left behind. Where was God in all this?"

Certainly her life wasn't fair. What once seemed sweet turned sour. A life begun in hope yielded only disappointment and pain. Lord, what do You expect of us in situations like this?

*See to it that no one falls short of the grace of God
and that no bitter root grows up
to cause trouble and defile many.*

HEBREWS 12:15 NIV

...let me never be put to shame...

Lord, why do I feel shame at being a widow? The very word makes me cringe. I did nothing to make myself a widow, nor did I choose to be one. Why do I feel shame if I'm not responsible?

Did being married carry such cachet for me that losing the title *wife* embarrasses me? I understand my grief. I understand my fear. I do not understand my feeling of shame.

Lord, I want to live in this unsought role in a way that never casts shame on Your name. I want to live as a widow who has taken refuge in You where there is no shame.

_____

_____

_____

_____

In you, LORD, I have taken refuge;
let me never be put to shame.

PSALM 71:1 NIV

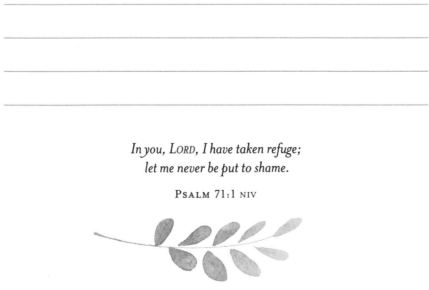

...the L'ORD sits enthroned...

"He always sat in the same spot," she says. Living rooms came and went, sofas came and went, but that particular spot was his for more than forty years. Every time she glances over, the emptiness is a blow to her heart.

The cat looks at her in question. Where is he? he seems to ask. I sat on his lap in our spot every night. Where am I supposed to sit now? She sighs and wipes away her tears.

When empty seats hollow us out and loss presses hard, remind us that You sit enthroned above the heavens, our King forever.

The L'ORD sits enthroned over the flood;
the L'ORD sits enthroned as king forever.
May the L'ORD give strength to his people!
May the L'ORD bless his people with peace!

PSALM 29:10-11

...all the days were written...

Lord, we stood around his bed holding his hand, singing to him. We didn't know if he was aware, but since hearing is the last sense to go, we told him how much we loved him. I smoothed his hair and kissed his cheek.

I thank You for this sweet memory. At the same time, I struggle with the idea that he had to go at all. I know You, as author and finisher of our faith, wrote our stories before we even began to live them. I'm just surprised and saddened by how soon You wrote him out of mine. Still, I choose to trust You.

---   .

All the days ordained for me were written in your book
before one of them came to be.

PSALM 139:16 NIV

...the faithful God who keeps covenant...

The word *faithful*, when used in the context of marriage, causes one of two reactions, Lord. There are those like me who thank You for a husband who was faithful, whether on the road or at home. Then there are those whose hearts were broken by the faithless ones they should have been able to trust the most.

Whether our relationships were fractured or fine, one truth upholds us all: You, O Lord, are faithful. Always. Whether the sun shines or the floods come, we don't have to worry about You leaving us. You are faithful yesterday, today, and forever.

Know therefore that the LORD your God is God,
the faithful God who keeps covenant and steadfast love
with those who love him and keep his commandments,
to a thousand generations.

DEUTERONOMY 7:9

...my flesh and my heart may fail...

The solitary bellow of a cow cuts the air. Living in Amish country, I see cows and horses all the time but rarely hear them, which is why this loud bawl catches my attention. It's a cry of bovine frustration.

I feel like bellowing too, Lord, bawling my frustration, my grief. I'm overwhelmed with big problems—my husband died!—and small ones—I forgot to take out the trash this week because it was his job in our little universe.

Know, Father, that despite my frustration, I choose to say, "I may fail, but You are my strength."

_My flesh and my heart may fail,
but God is the strength of my heart
and my portion forever._

PSALM 73:26

...tears in your bottle...

Why are some days weepier than others, Lord? I've tried to analyze what makes the difference, and I've come to no conclusion. I'm folding laundry or staring in the fridge trying to decide what to eat, and the tears begin.

And You collect my tears of loss like the ancients collected tears of pain and sorrow in literal bottles or tear vials. I'm too Western to want a bottle of tears to remind me of what I'll never forget, but what a comfort to know You remember my pain. You hold it close to Your heart. You understand!

_____

_____

_____

_____

You have kept count of my tossings;
put my tears in your bottle.
Are they not in your book?

PSALM 56:8

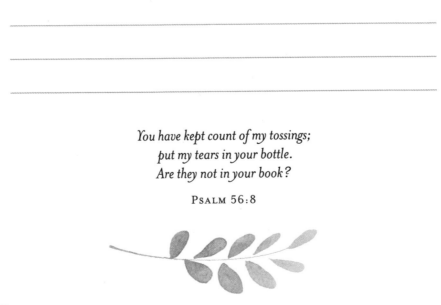

...I will uphold you with my righteous right hand...

Lord, being a wife was a huge part of who I am. It was a role I played with pride for many years. Now I'm no longer a wife, and I'm left with so many questions.

What do I do with the time I spent doing wifely things? Thinking wifely thoughts? What do I do with all my no-longer-needed love? Who will hold me? Who do I share my thoughts with? Where do I find an opinion I value as much as his?

How do I do being alone?

Please, Lord, help me. Give me strength. Hold me close. I need You.

*Fear not, for I am with you;
be not dismayed, for I am your God;
I will strengthen you, I will help you,
I will uphold you with my righteous right hand.*

Isaiah 41:10

...the LORD will fulfill his purpose...

We widows have questions, Lord. They aren't things like where did evil come from or how should we understand the Book of Revelation. Our questions are: Why him? Why now? Why our family? Why so suddenly and without warning? Why so slowly and with such pain?

But underneath these questions, those of us who love Jesus know that You, Father God, are in control despite our uncertainties. You are God Almighty, maker of heaven and earth, the One who asked Job, "Where were you when I laid the foundations of the earth?"

Job couldn't answer, and I can't answer my questions. Faith says I don't have to. I trust.

Job answered the LORD and said:
"I know that you can do all things,
and that no purpose of yours can be thwarted."

JOB 42:1-2

...he will make straight your paths...

Lord, everywhere I look, there are directions pointing the way. Follow the dots. Cook for fifteen minutes. Take two tablets. Turn left.

Sadly, there's no Google Maps or Waze for navigating my new and unknown paths. There's no TripTik with a convenient red line showing me the way. There's not even tiny print on a folded piece of paper in a hard-to-open bottle.

But there is the Word. There's prayer. There's You, Lord, and You want me to follow You even more than I want to follow You. Give me understanding, Lord. Show me Your path.

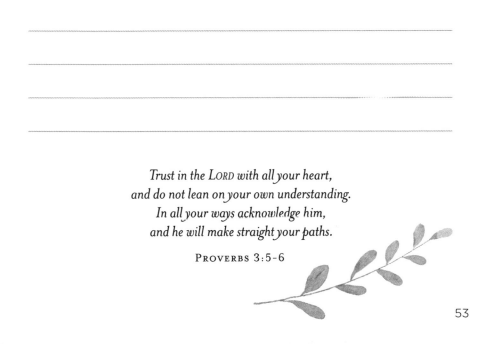

Trust in the LORD with all your heart,
and do not lean on your own understanding.
In all your ways acknowledge him,
and he will make straight your paths.

PROVERBS 3:5-6

53

...I am the one who helps...

Lord, I have a touch screen on my laptop. I love the convenience of not having to worry about a mouse, but I continually have a screen covered in fingerprints. I have a microfiber cloth that cleans away the prints quickly and easily, leaving an unmarred surface.

Grief isn't so easily erased, Lord. Its fingerprints are sticky and deface every surface they touch. No matter the depth of my faith and the strength of my trust in You, grief pervades my life. While I don't welcome it, I accept its presence. I know I can't avoid it.

But it won't turn me from You, Holder of my hand and Healer of my heart.

I, the LORD your God, hold your right hand;
it is I who say to you, "Fear not, I am the one who helps you."

ISAIAH 41:13

...*protector of widows*...

The hot water heater is leaking, Lord, and I'm without hot water. In a panic I call the plumbers who advertise on TV all the time. The price they quote makes me hyperventilate, and they can't come for three days. Help!

My friend calls, and I share my sad tale. She immediately tells me about a friend's son who is establishing his own business. I call and he will come immediately. His price is wonderful.

Now I have a new heater, hot water, and a wonderful young plumber. Thank You, Lord, for taking care of this widow.

_____

_____

_____

_____

Father of the fatherless and protector of widows
is God in his holy habitation.

PSALM 68:5

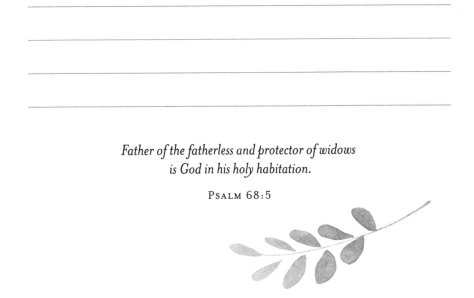

...let your steadfast love comfort me...

It constantly amazes me, Lord, how some small thing can set off a tidal wave of emotion. A whiff of Irish Spring, his favorite soap. A deep laugh from across the room. A plaid shirt just like his. The sight of a man in a crowd who has his body build, his haircut, his gait.

My breath catches. My heart skips a beat. Can it be?

Of course, it can't, but for that briefest of moments I want to believe.

Then reality bites deep. My eyes well with tears, and I'm doubly alone. Come close, Lord. I need You.

Let your steadfast love comfort me
according to your promise to your servant.
Let your mercy come to me, that I may live;
for your law is my delight.

PSALM 119:76-77

...let your good Spirit lead me...

Lord, I'm scared about my finances. When it was two of us, we managed to pay our bills every month, put a little away in savings, and even take vacations. Then he died, and I lost a significant amount of income. Unfortunately, I didn't lose my bills. I still have the mortgage, utilities, insurance, taxes, and more.

What should I do, Lord? Should I sell the house? Should I get a condo or rent an apartment? Should I buy a smaller home? Should I consider a retirement community?

I know this is not a right or wrong issue, but there is a better or best. Show me what's best for me.

_____

_____

_____

_____

Teach me to do your will, for you are my God!
Let your good Spirit lead me on level ground!

PSALM 143:10

...who apportions to each one individually...

I'm watching my friend, Lord, and I'm confused. Is she right, or am I?

She's been a widow for a shorter time than I have, but she doesn't seem to be wrestling with the stuff of everyday life like me. Am I doing something wrong? Should I be further along than I am? Or is she putting on a happy face and then crying in the privacy of her bedroom just like me?

Maybe it's a matter of personality as we both seek You in our grief. While we all bear Your image, we are all different. Not right. Not wrong. Just different.

All these are empowered by one and the same Spirit,
who apportions to each one individually as he wills.

1 CORINTHIANS 12:11

...*delight yourself in the* LORD...

Lord, the coffee table is big and square and garish. It has yellow and pink flowers with green leaves painted on an aqua background, and I can't believe I bought it. I'm Miss Conservative. Sure, I like bright colors. Red's my favorite with yellow right behind, but one color at a time and not in my furniture.

The table's for my new sunroom, its first piece of furniture. It's weird. It's atypical. It's a ray of sunshine in the grayness of my widowhood. It's a God-gift, the fulfillment of a desire I didn't even know I had. May I recognize all such gifts, Lord. Thanks.

Delight yourself in the LORD,
and he will give you the desires of your heart.

PSALM 37:4

...as white as snow...

Lord, I'm glad I didn't live in the Victorian Era. Widows were expected to wear unrelieved black for a year, then black with a bit of jewelry, probably jet, also black, for another year. Next came gray, graduating to lavender before other colors were allowed.

Grief doesn't need black clothing to be felt, noticed, or to overwhelm. It grabs hold and digs in its claws like the most vicious of beasts. If it wasn't for You, Lord, I'd be clothed in black spiritually, helpless and hopeless. Because of You, I'm held secure through my grief, washed white as snow.

_____

_____

_____

_____

Come now, let us reason together, says the LORD:
though your sins are like scarlet, they shall be as white as snow;
though they are red like crimson, they shall become like wool.

ISAIAH 1:18

...let not your hearts be troubled...

The air is dense with heavy rain. Lightning flashes and thunder rumbles, long, low growls rather than sharp claps. Trees bend beneath the wind, the leaves tumbling, churning. And the flowers! They droop and tear under the intensity of the downpour.

Grief is like this rain. It's drenching. Damaging. Relentless.

It's so easy to forget that He's the one who said to the storm, "Peace! Be still!" And the waters calmed. The winds ceased.

He can calm our stormy hearts, still the thunder and lightning of our grief. In the midst of the gale, He can give peace.

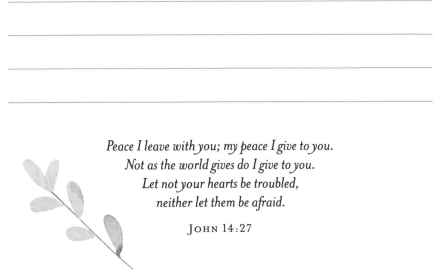

Peace I leave with you; my peace I give to you.
Not as the world gives do I give to you.
Let not your hearts be troubled,
neither let them be afraid.

John 14:27

...that the works of God might be displayed...

Lord, I'm angry, and I'm asking You what I did to deserve this pain.

Even as I think that, I check myself. I remember the man born blind. "Who sinned, this man or his parents, that he was born blind?" the disciples asked in John 9. Jesus replied that neither the man nor his parents had sinned, but it was for God's glory. And He healed the man.

Can my situation, my deep grief, also be for Your glory? Can my trust in You in the midst of my pain bring You praise? Oh, Lord, may Your works be displayed in me so others see You. It would be no less a miracle than the healing of the blind man.

_____

_____

_____

_____

Jesus answered, "It was not that this man sinned, or his parents, but that the works of God might be displayed in him."

JOHN 9:3

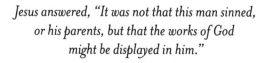

...eat and drink and find enjoyment...

Lord, I don't want to sit home and feel sorry for myself this Valentine's Day. Been there. Done that. Besides, why should couples be the only ones who get to enjoy the special menus created for this day?

Six of us women end up sitting down together: three widows, two never-marrieds, and a divorcee. We eat and laugh and have a delightful time, creating our own fun. Would I rather be celebrating with him? Of course. But Lord, you have gifted me with life and friends. I choose, with Your help, to learn to enjoy both.

_____

_____

_____

_____

Behold, what I have seen to be good and fitting is to eat and drink and find enjoyment in all the toil with which one toils under the sun the few days of his life that God has given him.

ECCLESIASTES 5:18

...they are new every morning...

Mornings are hard, Lord. There's that sweet moment before I glance at the pillow next to mine and realize it hasn't been slept on. The covers aren't disturbed. No body heat slips over to warm me. No arms wait to hold me.

All the loss rushes back, all the hurt, the loneliness, the grief. The day can be bright and golden with sunshine or overcast and gray with clouds. The stab of realization pierces regardless. Every morning.

Help me remember Your mercies are also new every morning, and they are mine to hold onto because of Your unfailing and steadfast love.

_____

_____

_____

_____

*The steadfast love of the L*ORD *never ceases;*
his mercies never come to an end;
they are new every morning; great is your faithfulness.

LAMENTATIONS 3:22-23

…behold, I am doing a new thing…

It's tax time, Lord, and for the first time I'm filing as a single. Do You hear me sigh?

I am facing many unexpected new things I'm not qualified or gifted for but must do anyway. Like my taxes. Like the lawn. Like caring for the car. Like managing the money. Like renewing the insurance. Like changing the light bulbs or reaching the top shelf.

When You said You were doing a new thing, You meant in the hearts of Your people, but, Lord, will You please do new things in the practical areas of my life too? Enable me to do more than I know how.

_____

_____

_____

_____

Behold, I am doing a new thing;
now it springs forth, do you not perceive it?
I will make a way in the wilderness and rivers in the desert.

Isaiah 43:19

…a tree planted by streams of water…

It's winter here, and the trees are stripped of their leaves. The branches spread gnarled fingers, black against a pearl gray sky. I remember when those same branches were alive with emerald, celadon, jade, hunter, veridian—an artist's palette of greens, rich and lush against the warm sapphire sky.

I used to be a leafy tree, Lord, alive and vibrant. Now I'm stripped of color and life. I'm left bereft, chilled. Remind me that this season of dormancy and loss is temporary even though it feels forever. By Your grace, may I one day leaf out again.

_____

_____

_____

_____

He is like a tree planted by streams of water
that yields its fruit in its season,
and its leaf does not wither.

PSALM 1:3

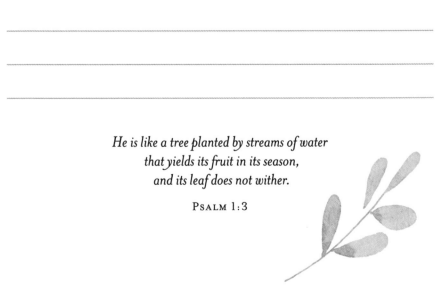

...my times are in your hand...

Lord, time is such a proof of Your existence. Where did it come from if not from Your hand? It doesn't hold the fractured logic of step-by-step evolution. You spoke, and time was.

Time is what keeps order, what allows history to unspool. It moves ever forward no matter what we do. We can't stop it. All we can do is live with its inevitable consequences.

Not that long ago time was my friend. I had an abundance of it to enjoy my husband, my marriage, my life. Then his time stopped, and my tidy little time capsule imploded. Creator of time, help!

I trust in you, O LORD; I say, "You are my God."
My times are in your hand.

PSALM 31:14-15

...my thoughts are not your thoughts...

"I'm not worried about you," he told me. "You'll be fine."

Questionable, but I took it as the great compliment it was.

"I'm just so sad I won't get to watch the grandkids grow up. I won't see who they become, who they marry, if they follow the Lord. I won't get to talk with them about their dreams, celebrate their accomplishments with them, and cry over their disappointments with them."

Lord, I wonder why You didn't give him that opportunity and the grandkids that great blessing. I'm choosing to trust that You know best even though I do not understand.

My thoughts are not your thoughts,
neither are your ways my ways, declares the LORD.
For as the heavens are higher than the earth,
so are my ways higher than your ways
and my thoughts than your thoughts.

ISAIAH 55:8-9

...He set my feet upon a rock...

Today's an earthquake day, Lord. I found out a terrible thing about someone close to me, and it will force unwanted changes on many lives, mine included. I'm hurt and shaken, and I'm struggling to keep my balance as my world once again heaves.

This new tragedy strikes just as I've started to feel my grief slowly healing. New shock waves of distress knock me sideways, and the rumble of my life's tectonic plates again shifting has me scrambling for solid footing.

I'm learning life can get better, but it can also get worse. Lord, be my Rock and my Security in this unstable world.

He drew me up from the pit of destruction,
out of the miry bog, and set my feet upon a rock,
making my steps secure.

Psalm 40:2

...for that is far better...

Lord, I would like him back, please. I want to take a walk with him. I want to sit quietly with him by the fire. I want to disagree with him on politics. I want to ask his opinion about the issue that's bothering me. I want to rest in his arms.

But that's selfish, isn't it? He's free of pain, of earth's restraints. He's enjoying Your presence. I don't understand all that means, Lord, but I do understand he should not come back. He would not want to come back. Help me rejoice for him in the part of my heart that is holding fast to what was but can never be again.

_____

_____

_____

_____

My desire is to depart and be with Christ,
for that is far better.

PHILIPPIANS 1:23

...*God lightens my darkness*...

It's night, Lord, and as I look outside my lighted room, all I see is black. I know there's a patio with a large planter out there. I know there's an oak tree that has finally gotten tall enough and leafy enough to give shade to the patio in the summer.

But all I see is black.

Grief causes me to see life as black, Lord, even though family and friends surround me, even though You are at my side. I know there is light even when all I see is dark. You are light, my light. Brighten my night. Pierce my darkness.

You are my lamp, O LORD,
and my God lightens my darkness.

2 SAMUEL 22:29

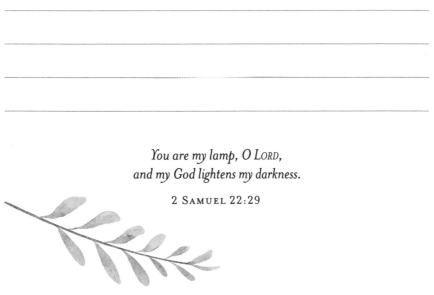

...*now to him who is able*...

Lord, I wonder if I told him how much I appreciated him. Sure, I told him I loved him, but did I say why? He was caring and careful, loving and loyal. He was responsible and respectful, fun and fair, and fiscally responsible. I wish I had told him more often how wonderful he was, but it's too late now.

But I can tell You, Lord. You are worthy and wonderful, glorious and giving. You put hope in my heart even in my pain, and You love me even when I sit crying in the corner. You are grace and grandeur, and You are my redeemer. I praise Your name.

Now to him who is able to do far more abundantly than all that we ask or think, according to the power at work within us, to him be glory in the church and in Christ Jesus throughout all generations, forever and ever. Amen.

EPHESIANS 3:20-21

...the LORD will fulfill his purpose for me...

Lord, I fear I've lost my way. Oh, not from You. You are the one sure thing in my life. It's just that I feel so useless. If I was a young widow, I'd have the purpose of caring for our children. If I was still working, I'd have my job to go to.

I'm an older widow. The kids are gone, and my nine-to-five days are behind me. But I still want to have purpose. I still want to serve You. It's amazing how long twenty-four hours can be without specific things to do. Teach me how I should fill this time, Lord. I'm trusting that You still have a plan for me.

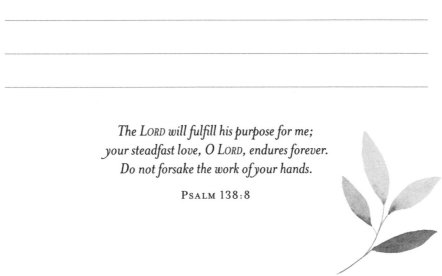

The LORD will fulfill his purpose for me;
your steadfast love, O LORD, endures forever.
Do not forsake the work of your hands.

PSALM 138:8

...because he holds fast to me...

Father, I love the loon with its black and white feathers, black head, and red eye. Hearing its mournful cry echo over a lake gives me chills. The parent loon floats with its young on its back and will not dive while a chick rides atop, even though diving is its main method of self-protection.

You are a protective parent, Father God. You carry me in my distress and destitution. You never leave me no matter the situation. You care for me not because I deserve Your loving protection, but simply because I am Yours through faith.

Because he holds fast to me in love,
I will deliver him; I will protect him,
because he knows my name.

PSALM 91:14

74

...train yourself for godliness...

Lord, I smile as I remember our first apartment, the thrill of sitting at our own table, and the intimacy of hanging our clothes in the same closet. I remember learning to respect his engineer precision while he learned to give me grace when I was less than precise. Learning to be a couple was challenging but fun.

Now I must learn to be an individual, also challenging but so not fun. Now come tears instead of smiles and confusion instead of excitement. I'm finding I can easily and naturally become self-oriented since there's no one here to think about but me.

Or there's another option: I can strive to become godly—which should always be my goal, married or single.

Have nothing to do with irreverent, silly myths.
Rather train yourself for godliness;
for...godliness is of value in every way,
as it holds promise for the present life
and also for the life to come.

1 TIMOTHY 4:7-8

...you are my rock and my fortress...

Lord, he was a man who kept things close to the vest. His wife didn't realize how close until he died suddenly, and she didn't know his passwords. She couldn't get into their finances, his computer, or his phone.

Talk about feeling helpless and lost. It wasn't merely shifting sand beneath her feet but quicksand about to swallow her whole. Over and over she prayed, "Help, Lord! I'm sinking."

I've prayed that same prayer as I faced my own shifting sands. How I thank You for being that rock of refuge to whom I can turn and upon which I can stand.

Be to me a rock of refuge, to which I may continually come;
you have given the command to save me,
for you are my rock and my fortress.

PSALM 71:3

...*I will confess my transgressions...*

Lord, if I had known the day he was leaving, would it have made a difference? Would I have been kinder, more attentive, more loving? Would I have gotten angry over what in hindsight was nothing of importance? Would I have done what he wanted instead of insisting on my way? Would I have swallowed that sharp retort?

I cannot change how I behaved no matter how much I wish I could, nor do I want to spend the rest of my life weighted with regret. I confess I am a sinner, Lord, and claim Your grace-filled promise of forgiveness.

_____

_____

_____

_____

I said, "I will confess my transgressions to the LORD,"
and you forgave the iniquity of my sin.

PSALM 32:5

...whose minds are steadfast...

I welcome the distraction of things that have no emotional cachet. HGTV. Animal videos. *Diners, Drive-Ins and Dives.* Guaranteed happily-ever-after novels or movies. I have no tolerance for anything that's sad or hard or depressing because my life is currently all these things, and I will not willingly invite more in.

How precious is the promise, Lord, that You will keep us in perfect peace if we fix our minds on You. Even as I use the distractions to fill the long evenings, I recognize they are merely fillers. You are the giver of grace and peace. You alone.

_____

_____

_____

_____

*You will keep in perfect peace
those whose minds are steadfast,
because they trust in you.*

ISAIAH 26:3 NIV

...we see in a mirror dimly...

Lord, I look more carefully at the windows of my lighted room, and I see not just the black outside but the reflections in the glass. I see the rocking chair, the bookcase, the African violet on the end table. It's a dim, wavering representation of the room's bright reality.

When we think of eternity, of heaven, we see only a dim reflection. Someday we'll see clearly. He sees fully now, doesn't he? He's more alive than he's ever been. Someday I'll be alive like that too. Give me grace and strength as I wait alone.

Now we see in a mirror dimly, but then face to face.
Now I know in part; then I shall know fully,
even as I have been fully known.

1 Corinthians 13:12

...the pleasing aroma of Christ...

In my linen closet two rows of bottles stand rank upon rank like little soldiers in pale blue uniforms. They're bath gels and body lotions in my favorite fragrance. Without asking my opinion, the company decided to cancel that fragrance, so I quickly bought a supply.

I find it a miracle, Father, that You consider us, your children, a pleasing fragrance. We aren't lined up like little bottles, similar and lifeless. Rather we're living beings with unique fragrances, the pleasing aromas of Christ to You. Even in my distress and with my questions, because of Jesus, I still please You.

We are to God the pleasing aroma of Christ among those who are being saved and those who are perishing.

2 Corinthians 2:15 niv

...tell to the coming generation...

"When we left the house for the first time after Dad's death, we drove down the street out of sight, stopped the car, and cried," our son tells me. "The fact that only you stood at the door broke our hearts."

It saddens me, Lord, that no matter how hard I try, I can't ease their grief. They loved him deeply. He encouraged them, adored them, advised them, and not only told them about Jesus, but also modeled what a godly man should be. Lord, may they honor his memory by being as gracious and faithful to their children as he was to them.

We will...tell to the coming generation
the glorious deeds of the LORD,
and his might, and the wonders that he has done.

PSALM 78:4

...I have called you by name...

I was proud to take his name when we married. It was a sign that we were now a unit, a single entity, a family. There was nothing of mastery on his part or giving up myself on my part. Rather it represented the truth that two are stronger than one. It meant us against the world. Then, too, his name was much easier to spell than my former one.

I may have lost the security of my marriage unit, Lord, but I am not nameless. You have called me by name. I am Yours. My name is written in Your book. I am both saved and safe.

_____

_____

_____

_____

Fear not, for I have redeemed you;
I have called you by name, you are mine.

Isaiah 43:1

...for God alone, O my soul...

Lord, as a widow I have to learn to steward my time and my emotions. I used to be strong and tireless, but now I only have so much stamina. I hope my fatigue will get better with time, but for now I claim the right to say no.

People don't always understand when I say no. Come on, they say, you need to get out. You need to get involved.

True, I do, but not on days I'm feeling fragile. While I don't want to hide behind #widowweeping, I must seek solitude with You to replenish my depleted strength. You alone can restore my soul.

For God alone, O my soul, wait in silence,
for my hope is from him.

PSALM 62:5

...he stores up sound wisdom...

Lord, I'm playing a video game where objects are hidden in something similar in color or shape. A trumpet is hidden in the yellow flames of the fire. A white flower rests against a white statue. As the timer counts down, I scramble to unscramble the mysteries of the picture.

I'm scrambling to find the familiar in the chaos of my life too. Patterns of many years are gone, and in their place are confusion and uncertainty. I hesitate where before I would have had a strong yea or nay. Only You have the key to the mystery my life has become. Share Your wisdom, Lord?

_____

_____

_____

_____

The LORD gives wisdom;
from his mouth come knowledge and understanding;
he stores up sound wisdom for the upright;
he is a shield to those who walk in integrity,

PROVERBS 2:6-7

...for God alone...

For some time after my husband died, I was aware of people's concern for me. They told me they were praying for me. They asked how I was doing. They were attentive. Even when they were merely being polite, I appreciated it.

Now everyone has gone back to their regularly scheduled programs like nothing of import happened. I can't blame them. Theirs was not the life that shifted on its axis. So, it's just You and me, Lord. You alone are the One I can depend on. Others may or may not be there for me, but You will always be my steadfast and dependable God.

He alone is my rock and my salvation,
my fortress; I shall not be greatly shaken.

Psalm 62:2

...unless the LORD builds the house...

Lord, one of my favorite vacation spots was completely destroyed by the great tidal surge of Hurricane Ian. The little cottage on the beach was Old Florida instead of shiny condo-heavy New Florida. It won't be rebuilt, at least not as it was, though someday something new will rise on that valuable piece of property on the Gulf of Mexico.

My life experienced a tidal surge too, Lord. The old was washed away, gone forever. Something new is slowly rising in its place. Master Builder, guide the placement of each nail and 2 x 4, each thought and plan, each step and stratagem.

Unless the LORD builds the house,
those who build it labor in vain.
Unless the LORD watches over the city,
the watchman stays awake in vain.

PSALM 127:1

...*forgetting what lies behind...*

Lord, I feel guilty when I start to feel better. It's like grief says, "You need me, kiddo. I'm the only one who keeps him alive for you. As long as you ache, you won't forget him. You start to hope, and he'll disappear."

I know that's a grievous lie. He won't ever leave me. But it's true that opening myself to hope will force him to stand aside so I can learn to live with less of him. This is both a harsh truth and the key to living fully again.

Jesus, give me the grace to press on.

One thing I do: forgetting what lies behind
and straining forward to what lies ahead,
I press on toward the goal for the prize
of the upward call of God in Christ Jesus.

PHILIPPIANS 3:13–14

...let your speech be always with grace...

"I told him I was furious at him," she said. "It was his fault I was going to be a widow. It was his fault that I was sad and scared. If he'd only just gone to the doctor when I told him to! I told him I'd never forgive him." Her shoulders sag. "I remember his face when I said that, and it haunts me."

Lord, I never said anything that brutal, but I didn't always give the encouragement I should or offer the support he needed. Words not spoken can hurt almost as much as the verbal knives. Forgive me.

_____

_____

_____

_____

Let your speech be always with grace,
seasoned with salt, that ye may know
how ye ought to answer every man.

COLOSSIANS 4:6 KJV

...God of all comfort...

I don't feel well, Lord. My temples throb, and I ache all over. I want to curl up and pull the covers over my head. I want to sob, but it'll hurt too much. But my greater pain is emotional. He's not here to call if I need help. He's not here to take me to the doctor's if I get worse. He's not here to pick up a prescription. He's not here.

Hold me, God of all comfort. Wrap your arms around me in my sorrow and pain and loneliness and say, "There, there, child. It'll be all right. I'm here."

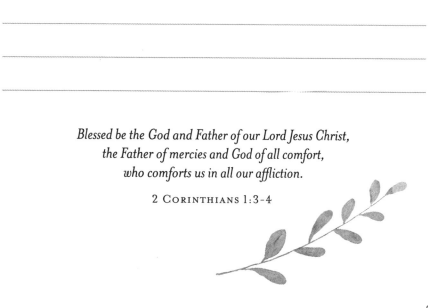

Blessed be the God and Father of our Lord Jesus Christ,
the Father of mercies and God of all comfort,
who comforts us in all our affliction.

2 Corinthians 1:3-4

...your God will come...

A brown leather lounge chair,
waiting, mocking, reminding
I am no longer wife
but widow.
The man who sat in it
is dancing with Jesus
while I weep alone
in the night.
Strengthen my feeble hands.
Steady my knees that give way.
"Be strong, my child; do not fear.
I have come."

_____

_____

_____

_____

Strengthen the feeble hands, steady the knees that give way;
say to those with fearful hearts, "Be strong, do not fear;
your God will come...he will come to save you."

ISAIAH 35:3-4 NIV

...for as in Adam all die...

Lord, some days I get very angry at Adam. Not Adam down the street but Adam, the first man. And Eve, of course. If they hadn't eaten that forbidden fruit, there wouldn't be death. I'm not sure how that would have worked. Would there have been no aging? What about overpopulation if no one died?

Useless questions because they did eat the fruit and ruin it all. As a result, my husband is dead, and I'm left with pain and sorrow. I know being angry at Adam is a foolish waste of time. Rather, Lord Jesus, help me rejoice because I have life in You.

For as in Adam all die,
so also in Christ shall all be made alive.

1 CORINTHIANS 15:22

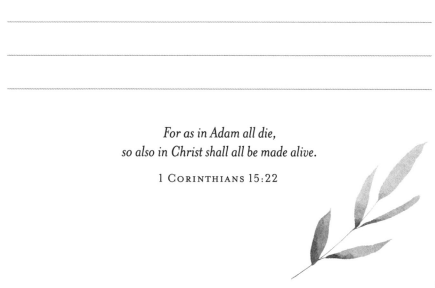

...I will instruct you and teach you...

Lord, I often pass by a house that had a terrible fire months ago. The roof is gone, the walls are distended and broken, the windows blown out. Nothing has been done to demolish what can clearly never be rebuilt.

It's a warning to me of what I can become after the ravages of the great emotional fire that swept through my life. I can deteriorate under the weight of my sorrow and despair, or I can choose to reconstruct a new life and find a new purpose.

Show me how to reconstruct my life, Lord. Please teach me how to rebuild.

I will instruct you and teach you in the way you should go;
I will counsel you with my eye upon you.

PSALM 32:8

...he shall not be cast headlong...

The geese are landing at the nearby pond, honking loudly as they descend, wings arced to slow their speed. Their feet hit the water with a splash and disappear beneath. Their bellies glide across the surface, serene and calm.

Lord, I'm like an unruly goose madly honking, flailing her wings as she falls, trying to control her life-flight in spite of being buffeted by the winds of fear and grief. I'm afraid I'll never have a safe landing or a smooth glide through life again. Remind me that I won't fall headlong because You are holding my hand.

Though he fall, he shall not be cast headlong,
for the LORD upholds his hand.

PSALM 37:24

...I will sing as long as I live...

Lord, what was once a duet has become a solo, and I don't want to sing my life's song alone. I don't know how. My voice is weak by itself. It's meant to blend, to harmonize. But the bass that ran beneath and strengthened my soprano has faded to silence.

I know I must continue to sing. I'm still alive. But how do I learn the notes for my new song? Where do I find the music? What if I sing the wrong notes?

Or is it as simple as I sing, and You teach me the new song as I go? A lesson in trust.

I will sing to the LORD as long as I live;
I will sing praise to my God while I have being.

PSALM 104:33

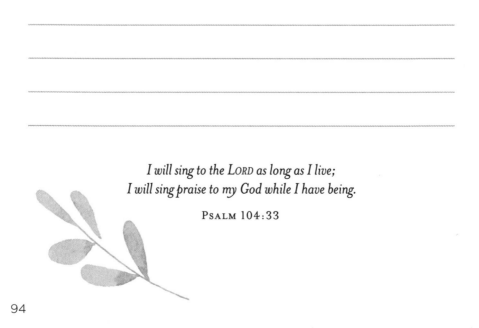

...who seek him with their whole heart...

In the ceiling of the master bedroom in this house, which I never shared with my husband, is a round disk covering the hole where a ceiling fan could hang. If he were still alive, there'd be a fan in that opening. He liked ceiling fans. We had them in previous homes.

I don't care for air blowing down on me, but I never objected. I didn't dislike it enough to make an issue of it. Compromise, right, Lord? Makes the marriage world go around.

But my spiritual world? May I never compromise in my wholehearted devotion to You.

_____

_____

_____

_____

Blessed are those who keep his testimonies,
who seek him with their whole heart.

PSALM 119:2

...let the meditation of my heart...

I'm getting casual about things since my husband died, Lord. I do what I want when I want. I go where I want when I want.

He wouldn't have liked that. He liked order, not in an obsessive, make-my-life-miserable way, but in an engineer way. He went to bed when it was bedtime, turned off the lights when he left the room, and mowed the grass on a schedule. Now, with only me to consider...well, it's different.

One thing I don't want to get casual about, Lord, is my relationship with You. I choose to seek You, not because I have to, but because I want to. You are my rock and my redeemer.

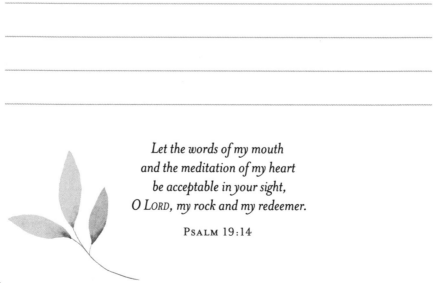

*Let the words of my mouth
and the meditation of my heart
be acceptable in your sight,
O Lord, my rock and my redeemer.*

PSALM 19:14

...I will never leave you nor forsake you...

Lord, I was at a concert the other night. The music was popular songs from my era, lots of fun to sing along. Suddenly they sang "our song." Boom! Just like that, tears. I remembered our romantic night all those years ago, the hope, the promise, the love. And it's all gone because he's gone.

These sneak attacks never fail to wound me, wind me. Oh, I recover more quickly than I used to, but they still remind me of all I've lost. Thank You, Lord, that our song—Yours and mine—will never end because You are ever present.

He has said, "I will never leave you nor forsake you."
So we can confidently say, "The Lord is my helper;
I will not fear; what can man do to me?"

HEBREWS 13:5-6

...I will remember...

I drove past that burned-out house yesterday, Lord, and a car was in the driveway. Someone is finally facing the catastrophe.

How do I face my catastrophe, Lord? I've never been in a situation like this before, so alone and broken. But I have been in hard situations before. I have been hurt. I have been disappointed. What did I do then? I turned to You, and You were there.

This situation is harder, the pain is deeper, but You are still with me. I will recall Your past care and trust You for my needs today and tomorrow.

I will remember the deeds of the LORD;
yes, I will remember your wonders of old.
I will ponder all your work,
and meditate on your mighty deeds.

PSALM 77:11-12

…may the God of hope fill you…

As I was driving this morning, Lord, two cars backed out of their neighboring driveways. I saw them; they should have seen me. I don't know where they were looking—perhaps at each other?—but I and the school bus coming from the opposite direction had to stop for them. Full stop.

My relationship with grief is like this. I'm driving along, doing fairly well, choosing hope, when grief unexpectedly sticks its rear end in my path. My forward progress is halted, at least temporarily. Lord, help me to choose hope found in You when grief tries to block my way.

May the God of hope fill you
with all joy and peace in believing,
so that by the power of the Holy Spirit
you may abound in hope.

ROMANS 15:13

...here a little, there a little...

"Does it ever get better?" she asked.

Lord, thank You that I can honestly say it does. Oh, not quickly and not for a long time. No matter how much I long for a quick resolution to my sorrow, a return to my previous emotional landscape, I am learning to accept that grief is as speedy as an inch worm crossing my garden.

In fact, it's such a slow process it's easy to miss "better" unless I look back and gauge today against where I was a year ago or two years ago. Lord, continue to move me forward inch by steady inch.

_____

_____

_____

_____

It is precept upon precept, precept upon precept,
line upon line, line upon line, here a little, there a little.

ISAIAH 28:10

...*praise his name with dancing*...

It was a large New Year's Eve gathering at a retirement community, Lord. Everything was fine through dinner. Then music began and couples rose to dance. "I felt a sledgehammer to my heart," she said. Never again would he hold her like that. Never again would they sway to the rhythm of a song. Never again.

A widow has to learn to dance again, Lord. She has to learn a new melody, move to an unfamiliar rhythm, sing a different lyric. It takes time to realize this new dance can also be joyous if You are our partner. May my feet move in step with Yours.

Let them praise his name with dancing,
making melody to him with tambourine and lyre!

PSALM 149:3

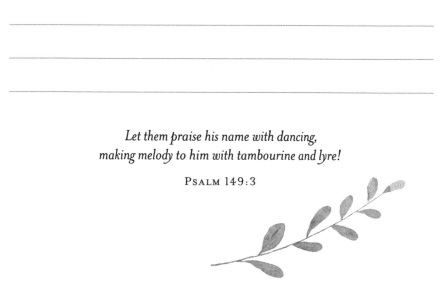

...they flourish...

Lord, my word for the year is flourish. I picked it as a challenge. I want to do more than merely manage life—which is all I was capable of for a while. But I'm slowly healing.

My goals aren't particularly high. It's more a matter of moving steadily forward than reaching great heights. If all I do is hand out bulletins at church, that's flourishing when before all I did was sit and grieve.

Lord, help me remember Your desire for me is that I live abundantly even in my heartache. I want to flourish in and for Your glory.

The righteous...are planted in the house of the LORD;
they flourish in the courts of our God.
They still bear fruit in old age;
they are ever full of sap and green.

PSALM 92:12-14

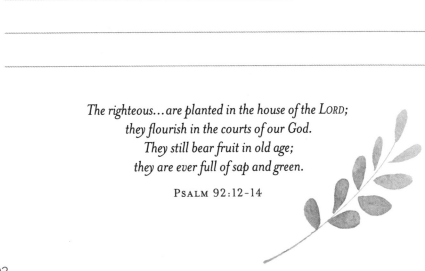

...therefore I will hope...

Lord, every time I turn around, I see something that makes me think of him. I wear the opal ring he gave me. I sit in his lounge chair when I watch TV. His face still smiles at me from family photos.

My heart hitches at these visual reminders, but it also rejoices. The photos especially recall good times. Easter egg hunts in the backyard. Thanksgiving gathered around the dining room table. Rowdy times with everyone throwing clumps of Christmas wrapping paper at each other and me finding a renegade clump of paper under the sofa in July.

Recalling happy times gives me hope, Lord. I choose hope—hope in You, hope in life.

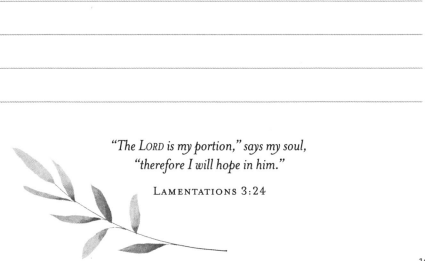

"The Lord is my portion," says my soul,
"therefore I will hope in him."

LAMENTATIONS 3:24

...to us who are being saved...

Lord, the little stuffed critter has a red plush body, a silly smile, and wings that are white with red hearts. When I press its tummy, it whistles like a construction worker whistles at a pretty girl. It makes me smile every time I hear it.

He and our young granddaughter gave it to me for a silly Valentine's gift many years ago, and it's a symbol of their love for me.

Symbols are so powerful, and the cross is the most powerful symbol of all to those of us who believe. Lord, may it ever remind me of Your power and love.

_____

_____

_____

_____

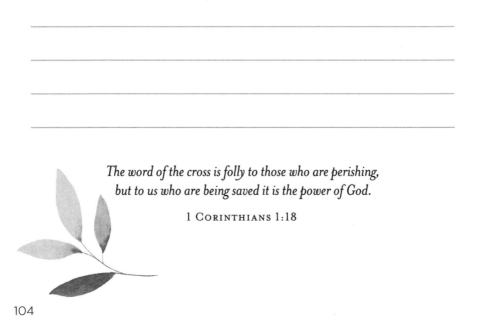

The word of the cross is folly to those who are perishing,
but to us who are being saved it is the power of God.

1 CORINTHIANS 1:18

...because you are my help...

Sunday morning, Lord, the service started with a beautiful solo. Not everyone realized the service had begun because the soloist chose to stay seated. An unaware woman behind me kept talking softly to her neighbor, and she became like a low frequency hum beneath the song.

Grief has become like that, Lord, an annoying low hum trying to disrupt me even though time has passed, and I'm beginning to do better. "Don't forget me," it says. "I'm your good friend. Keep your ears tuned to me, not that lovely song of life and hope you're beginning to hear. You need me."

But I don't. I need You.

_____

_____

_____

_____

Because you are my help,
I sing in the shadow of your wings.
I cling to you; your right hand upholds me.

PSALM 63:7-8 NIV

...underneath are the everlasting arms...

Lord, when I became a widow, it felt like a huge hole opened beneath my feet, and I found myself falling, falling. The sides of this great hole were jagged and ragged, and they tore at me as I fell. I was bruised and bleeding and in pain.

That hole remains and always will, but time has filed down the jagged edges that once pierced my heart, leaving me wounded and wondering. I've learned not to fear the hole because, no matter how far I fall, I will never be in free fall. Your arms, O Lord, are always stretched to catch me.

_____

_____

_____

_____

The eternal God is your dwelling place,
and underneath are the everlasting arms.

DEUTERONOMY 33:27

...see, the Lion...worthy is the Lamb...

The sunset is a soft lavender with pink streaks tonight. No flaming glory. Just gentle beauty. I need gentle, dear Lamb of God, after the drama and heartache of his death. Your invitation to come and find rest is a balm to my bruised heart.

Then the gentle sunset becomes a brilliant streak of red and gold and purple burning along the horizon. I'm reminded of Your boldness, Your power, O Lion of the tribe of Judah. When I need You to be my strength, You are.

Lamb and Lion. Lion and Lamb. The One who soothes and the One who strengthens. My Savior.

See, the Lion of the tribe of Judah,
the Root of David, has triumphed.
Worthy is the Lamb, who was slain.

REVELATION 5:5, 12 NIV

EPILOGUE

"Someday you will read in the papers that my husband is dead.
Don't you believe a word of it!
At that moment he shall be more alive than he ever was;
he shall have gone up higher."

—**GAYLE ROPER,** adapting D.L. Moody

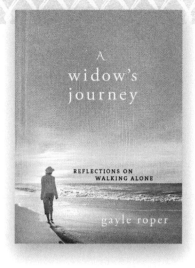

A widow's journey

REFLECTIONS ON
WALKING ALONE

gayle roper

When You Lose Your Husband...

"So who am I now that there's only one place at the table...one pillow with a head dent, one damp towel after a shower. There's only one toothbrush in the holder. The seat is never left up anymore. I can still write Mrs. in front of my name, but I'm no longer in a marriage relationship. You need two people for a marriage, and there's only me."

Is there only *you*? Then join Gayle as she draws on her emotions during the loss of her beloved husband, Chuck, and offers you a compassionate devotional to encourage you through your darkest days. Gayle knows a widow's pain is deep. But she also knows God's love is deeper still. And it's in His love you'll find your deepest comfort.

To learn more about Harvest House books and
to read sample chapters, visit our website:

www.HarvestHousePublishers.com

HARVEST HOUSE PUBLISHERS
EUGENE, OREGON